Seasons

Spring
Patricia Whitehouse

Heinemann Library
Chicago, Illinois

©2003 Reed Educational & Professional Publishing
Published by Heinemann Library,
an imprint of Reed Educational & Professional Publishing
Chicago, IL

Customer Service 888-454-2279
Visit our website at www.heinemannlibrary.com

Designed by Sue Emerson, Heinemann Library
Printed and bound in China by South China Printing Company

09
10 9 8 7 6 5

Library of Congress Cataloging-in-Publication Data
Whitehouse, Patricia, 1958–
     Spring / Patricia Whitehouse.
        v. cm. — (Seasons)
Includes index.
Contents: What are seasons?—What is the weather like in spring?—What do you wear in spring?—What can you see in spring?—What can you smell in spring?—What can you hear in spring?—What can you taste in spring?—What can you feel in spring?
     ISBN: 978-1-58810-894-4 (1-58810-894-5) (HC), ISBN: 978-1-4034-0540-1 (1-4034-0540-9) (Pbk)
     1. Spring—Juvenile literature. [1. Spring.] I. Title. II. Seasons
(Heinemann Library)
QB637.5 .W45 2003
508.2—dc21

                                    2002001164

Acknowledgments
The author and publishers are grateful to the following for permission to reproduce copyright material:
pp. 4, 5 J. A. Kraulis/Masterfile; p. 6L Paul Conklin/PhotoEdit; p. 6R Richard Hutchings/Photo Researchers, Inc.; p. 7 Robert Brenner/PhotoEdit; p. 8 Elizabeth Zuckerman/PhotoEdit; p. 9 Ariel Skelley/Corbis Stock Market; p. 10 Richard Smith/Masterfile; p. 11L Gale Zucker/Stock Boston; p. 11R Tim Davis/Stone/Getty Images; p. 12 Nance S. Trueworthy /Stock Boston; p13T R. J. Erwin/Photo Researchers, Inc.; p. 13B Jeff Lepore/Photo Researchers, Inc.; p. 14 Myrleen Ferguson/PhotoEdit; p. 15 Zefa Visual Media/Index Stock Imagery, Inc.; p. 16L Brock May/Photo Researchers, Inc.; p. 16R Jim Steinberg/Photo Researchers, Inc.; p. 17 Deborah Davis/Photo Edit; p. 18L Charles Gold/Corbis Stock Market; p. 18R Ned Therrien/AG Pix; p. 19 (row 1, L-R) Dennis Gottlieb/Foodpix, Steve Cole/PhotoDisc/PictureQuest; p. 19 (row 2, L-R) Stacy Pick/Stock Boston, Eisenhut & Mayer/Foodpix; p. 20L Comstock Images; p. 20R Rommel/Masterfile; p. 21T David Young-Wolff/PhotoEdit; p. 21B Eyewire Collection; p. 22 (row 1, L-R) Comstock Images, Visuals Unlimited; p. 22 (row 2, L-R) Jack Ballard/Visuals Unlimited, Rommel/Masterfile; p. 22 (row 3, L-R) Richard Smith/Masterfile, Jeff Greenberg/ Visuals Unlimited; p.23 (row 1, L-R) Tim Davis/Stone/Getty Images, Ned Therrien/AG Pix; p. 23 (row 2, L-R) Charles Gold/Corbis Stock Market, Nance S. Trueworthy/Stock Boston; p. 23 (row 3, L-R) Sue Emerson/Heinemann Library, Gale Zucker/Stock Boston; p. 23 (row 4) Jeff Lepore/Photo Researchers, Inc.

Cover photograph by Jim Cummins/Getty Images
Photo research by Scott Braut

Special thanks to our advisory panel for their help in the preparation of this book:
Eileen Day, Preschool Teacher
Chicago, IL

Ellen Dolmetsch, MLS
Wilmington, DE

Kathleen Gilbert,
Second Grade Teacher
Austin, TX

Sandra Gilbert,
Library Media Specialist
Houston, TX

Angela Leeper,
Educational Consultant
North Carolina Department
of Public Instruction

Raleigh, NC

Pam McDonald,
Reading Teacher
Winter Springs, FL

Melinda Murphy,
Library Media Specialist
Houston, TX

Some words are shown in bold, **like this.**
You can find them in the picture glossary on page 23.

Contents

What Is Spring?

| spring | summer |

Spring is a season.

There are four seasons in a year.

fall

winter

In most places, each season brings
new things to see and do.

5

What Is the Weather Like in Spring?

Spring is a changing season.

Weather changes from cold to warm.

It can be windy in spring.

It rains a lot, too.

What Do You Wear in Spring?

When it rains, you need clothes that keep you dry.

A raincoat can keep you dry.

On warm days you can wear shorts and a T-shirt.

What Can You Feel in Spring?

You can feel soft, new grass growing.

You can feel warm air on your skin.

You can feel the soft hair of a baby goat.

You can touch a soft baby **chick**.

What Can You See in Spring?

You can see flowers blooming in the spring.

These flowers are called **tulips**.

You can see birds building **nests.**

You can see **robins** looking for worms.

What Can You Smell in Spring?

You can smell flowers that are in bloom.

You can smell new grass.

You can smell the dirt after it rains.

What Can You Hear in Spring?

You can hear birds singing.

You can hear the breeze blowing in the trees.

You can hear rain falling.

You might hear thunder booming.

What Can You Taste in Spring?

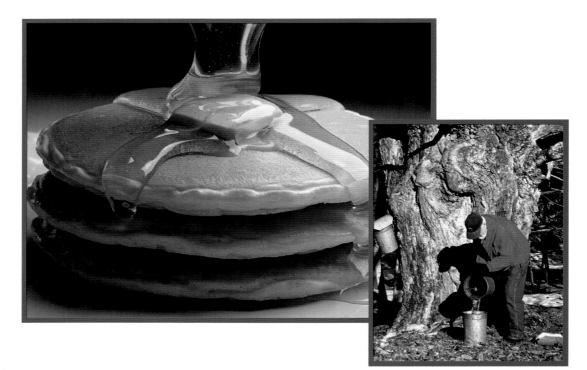

You can taste **maple** **syrup**.

It is made of **sap** from a maple tree.

lettuce

Easter candy

matzoh

asparagus

You can taste special spring foods.

What Special Things Can You Do in Spring?

You can fly a kite on a windy day.

You can pick spring flowers.

You can make presents for Mother's Day.

You can see a parade on Memorial Day.

Quiz

What can you do in the spring?

Picture Glossary

chick
page 11

robin
page 13

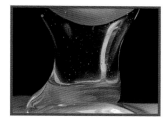
maple syrup
page 18

sap
page 18

nest
page 13

tulip
page 12

Note to Parents and Teachers

Reading for information is an important part of a child's literacy development. Learning begins with a question about something. Help children think of themselves as investigators and researchers by encouraging their questions about the world around them. Each chapter in this book begins with a question. Read the question together. Look at the pictures. Talk about what you think the answer might be. Then read the text to find out if your predictions were correct. Think of other questions you could ask about the topic, and discuss where you might find the answers. Assist children in using the picture glossary and the index to practice new vocabulary and research skills.

Index